A TOWER OF GIRAFFES

For

Isabella

Copyright © 2025 by Stephanie Lipsey-Liu.
All rights reserved
No part of this publication may be reproduced or transmitted in any form or by any means, electronic or mechanical, including photocopying, recording, scanning or otherwise, or through any information browsing, storage or retrieval system, without permission in writing from the publisher.

First printed 2025

ISBN 978-1-917565-07-3
Little Lion Publishing UK
Nottingham, England
www.littlelionpublishing.co.uk

The collective nouns you are about to learn are the real names for each group of animals! Some groups even have more than one name. Happy learning!

This Little Lion book belongs to

....

A prickle of porcupines

A prickle of porcupines trots down the track,
Keeping together with quills on their back.

Porcupines are rodents, just like rats, hamsters, and squirrels. They are some of the biggest rodents in the world! Even though they are both prickly, porcupines are not related to hedgehogs.

Porcupines are herbivores, which means they eat leaves, plants, twigs, and bark.. They have sharp quills all over their bodies to protect themselves.

Baby porcupines are called porcupettes!

African porcupines live on the ground, while American porcupines live up in trees.

Porcupines even make a singing noise that sounds a bit like a crying baby!

A tower of giraffes

A tower of giraffes strides gracefully slow,
Watching the world from heights we can't know.

Giraffes are the tallest animals in the world. An adult male giraffe can grow up to five and a half metres tall. Being tall, along with having good eyesight, helps them look out for predators.

Giraffes are herbivores, so they only eat plants. Their favourite food is the acacia tree!

A giraffe's tongue can grow as long as 53 cm! This helps them reach leaves high up in trees.

Giraffes get so much water from the food they eat that they only need to drink once every few days.

A tower of giraffes usually has around 15 members. They are led by one male, while the rest are females or young males.

A snuggle of sloths

A snuggle of sloths moves slow as can be,
Dozing on branches high up in the tree.

Sloths are either two-toed or three-toed. Two-toed sloths have two claws on their front legs, while three-toed sloths have three. They all have three claws on their back legs.

Sloths are folivores, a type of herbivore that feeds mainly on leaves. Sloths also eat some tree sap and fruit.

Sloths spend most of their lives hanging in trees. They only come down about once a week to poop!

Can you remember what a group of porcupines is called? Turn back to page 1 to see if you were right!

A dazzle of zebras

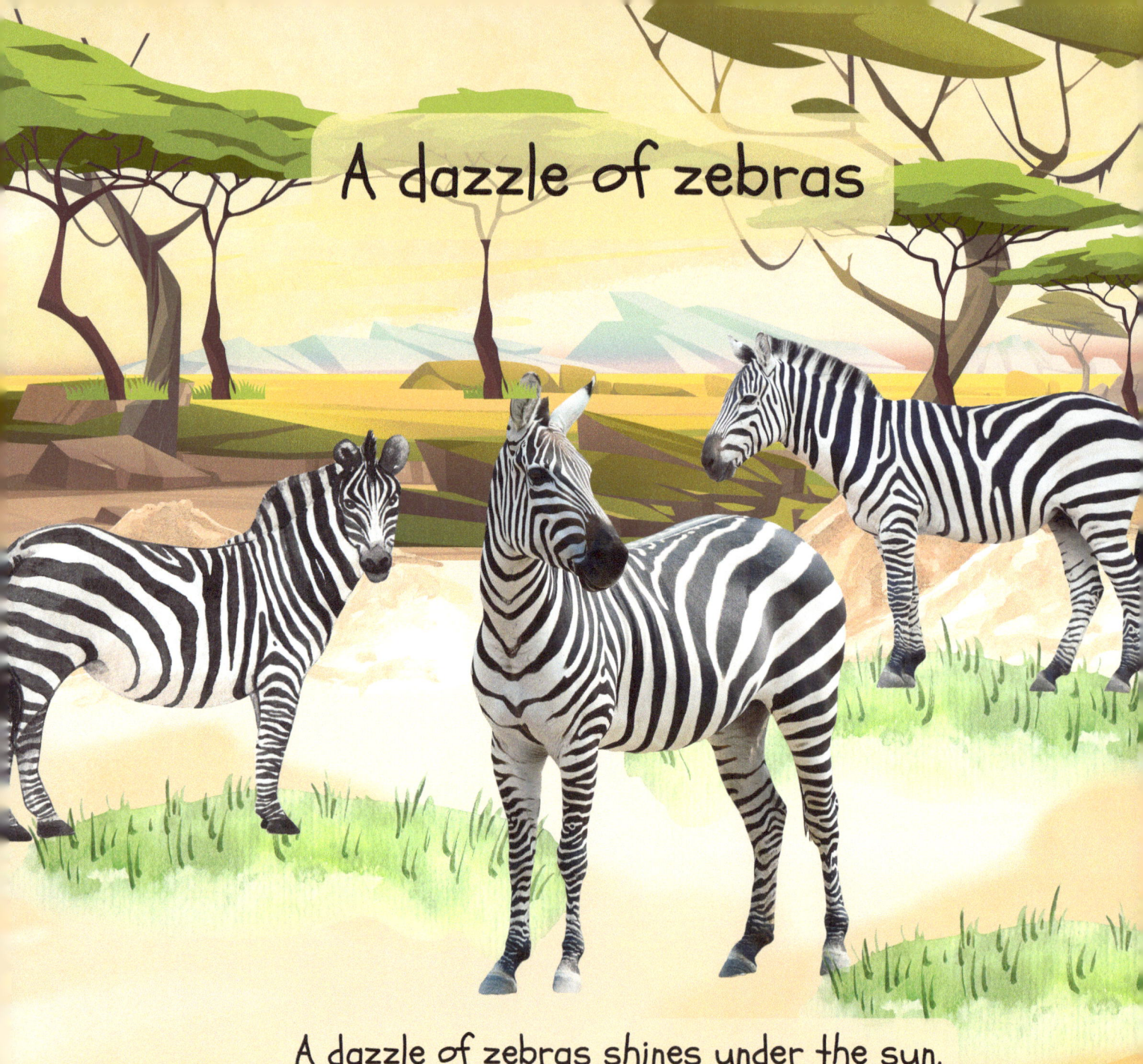

A dazzle of zebras shines under the sun,

Blending together yet ready to run.

Zebras are black with white stripes, not the other way around! They even have black skin under their hair, too.

A group of zebras is called a dazzle, or sometimes a herd. When zebras migrate, they often join into super herds with thousands together.

Zebras often defend younger or weaker members of the dazzle. They form a protective circle to fight off predators.

Zebra stripes may protect them from being bitten by flies! The stripes confuse the flies, making it hard for them to land.

Zebras can run up to 36 mph, which is faster than a lion!

Can you remember what a group of giraffes is called? Turn back to page 3 to see if you were right!

Rhinos are called "white" or "black" rhinos, but both are actually grey! English explorers misunderstood the word "wyd," which meant wide, as the word white. "Wyd" referred to their wide upper lip. The other rhinos were then called black because of this. Black rhinos have a pointy upper lip.

Rhinos can weigh over 3 tonnes!

Rhinos can't see very well, but they have an excellent sense of smell!

Rhino horns are made of keratin, the same material as our fingernails and toenails! Their horns grow throughout their lives, usually about 7 cm each year.

Male rhinos are called bulls, females are called cows and baby rhinos are called calves.

Can you remember what a group of sloths is called? Turn back to page 5 to see if you were right!

A caravan of camels

A caravan of camels keeps steady and strong,

Travelling the pathways that stretch far and long.

Camels have long eyelashes to protect their eyes from sand and they can also close their nostrils to keep the sand out.

Arabian camels have one hump and Bactrian camels have two. The humps are used to store fat. By not having fat all over their body, camels can keep cool.

Camels don't have hooves. They have two large toes that spread out to help them walk on the sand.

When a camel walks, the legs on the same side move together; both left legs then both right legs. Giraffes walk like this too.

Can you remember what a group of zebras is called? Turn back to page 7 to see if you were right!

There are three types of elephants:
1. The African Savanna Elephant
2. The African Forest Elephant
3. The Asian Elephant (with smaller ears)

The African Savanna Elephant is the largest land animal. They aren't fully grown until they are around 35-40 years old! They live for up to 70 years in the wild.

Elephants have 17 muscles in their trunks. They can breathe and smell through their trunks. They can suck water up their trunks and squirt it into their mouths, but they can't drink through them.

Elephants have wrinkly skin to help them stay cool. They take regular dust and mud baths to protect their skin from the sun.

Elephant tusks are actually teeth that continue growing their whole lives! They help them to dig for food and to fight.

Can you remember what a group of rhinos is called? Turn back to page 9 to check if you were right!

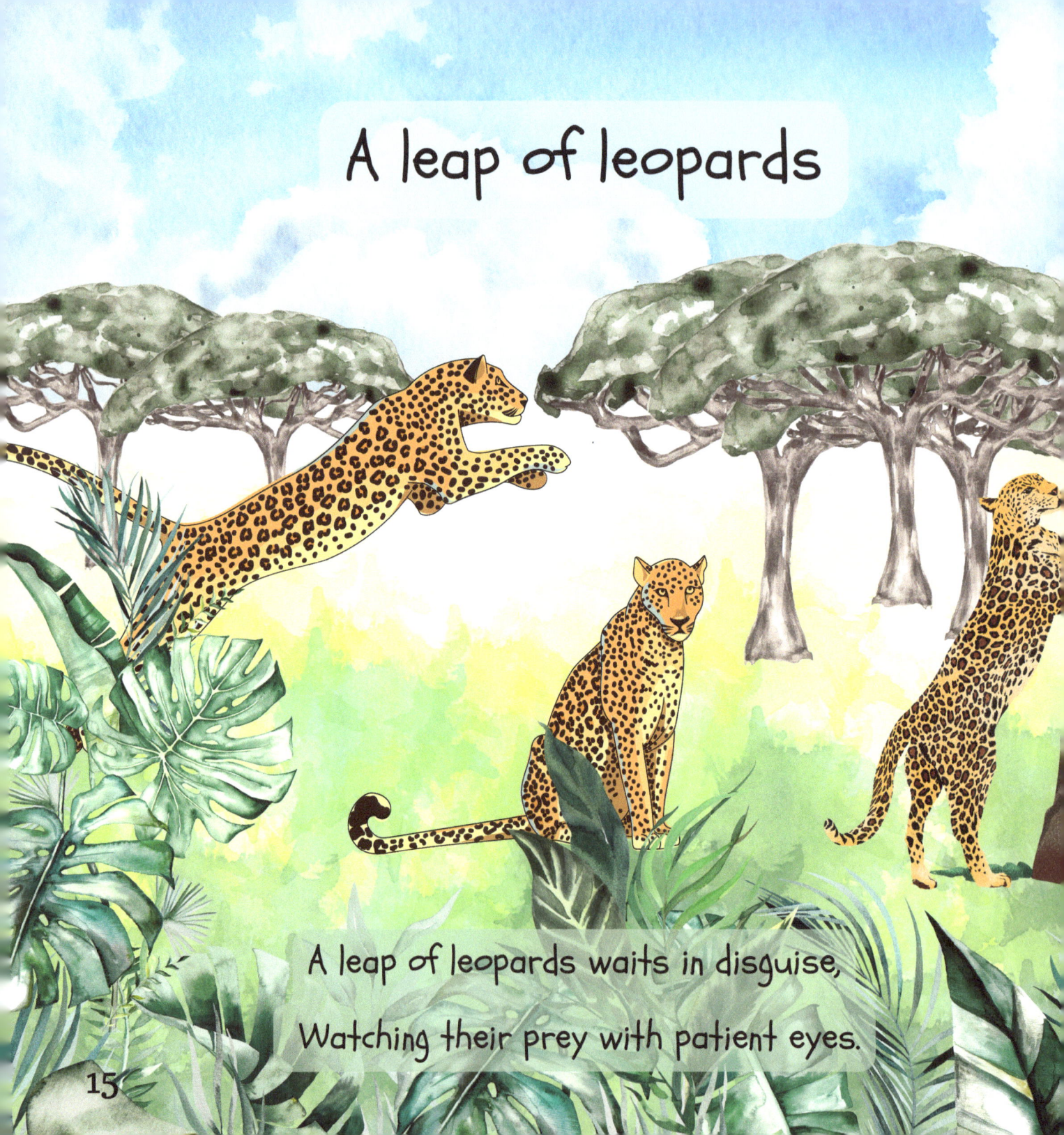

Leopard spots are called "rosettes" because they look like roses. Leopards all have different patterns of spots. The spots help leopards blend into the leaves around them so they can stalk their prey.

Leopards can leap as far as six metres!

Leopards often take their food up into the trees to stop hyenas and jackals from trying to steal it! They can carry animals that weigh more than themselves!

Leopards don't usually hang out in groups, so you're unlikely to ever see a leap of leopards. They only really come together to mate.

Can you remember what a group of camels is called? Turn back to page 11 to check if you were right!

A mess of iguanas

A mess of iguanas sprawls in the heat,
Stretching out tails and long scaly feet.

Some iguanas can regrow their tails. If a predator grabs an iguana by its tail, the iguana detaches its tail and escapes! If it was a clean break and the iguana is healthy, it can regrow its tail over the next year.

Green iguanas have a third eye! It is on top of their heads and can detect light and dark. This helps them detect predators from above and regulate their sleep.

Iguanas are great swimmers and can hold their breath for 30 minutes or more underwater.

Iguanas mainly eat leaves or algae. They spend most of their lives in trees.

Iguanas can grow up to 2 m long!

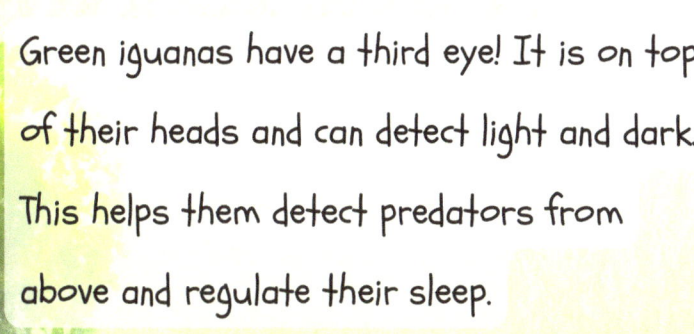

Can you remember what a group of elephants is called? Turn back to page 13 to check if you were right!

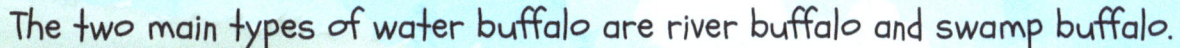
The two main types of water buffalo are river buffalo and swamp buffalo.

Water buffalo spend a lot of time in water or mud. This is because they can't sweat much, so they need to cool down in water.

Water buffalo have been helping humans for 5,000 years! They are useful in farming for pulling equipment, and also provide milk and meat.

Buffalo can run as fast as 30 miles per hour!

Can you remember what a group of leopards is called? Turn back to page 15 to check if you were right!

A stench of skunks

A stench of skunks explores in the night,

Glowing eyes twinkle in silver moonlight.

Skunks really do stink! If they feel threatened, they release a very smelly liquid from near their bottom! This is where their collective noun, a stench, comes from.

Skunks are nocturnal and rarely come out in the daytime.

A small number of people can't smell skunk spray—lucky them!

Skunks make dens to live in, or if they find an abandoned den from another animal, they will move in!

Skunks eat bugs, berries, nuts, bird eggs; just about anything they can find.

Can you remember what a group of iguanas is called? Turn back to page 17 to check if you were right!

A flight of dragons

A flight of dragons guards treasures untold,
Stories of wonder and legends of old.

Myths about dragons may have come from the fact that many people are afraid of snakes. The tales of dragons may have been told to children to stop them from straying too far from home.

The word "dragon" comes from the Greek word "drakon," which means serpent or giant sea fish.

Dragons are mentioned in tales all across the world.

In the West, dragons are said to be dangerous beasts that breathe fire and cause destruction. In the East, they are good creatures that bring luck. They don't have wings but can live in water.

 Can you remember what a group of water buffalo is called? Turn back to page 19 to check if you were right!

Glossary

Acacia tree – A type of tree that giraffes like to eat.

African Savanna Elephant – The largest land animal, with big ears and long tusks.

African Forest Elephant – A smaller type of African elephant that lives in forests.

Algae – Tiny plants that can grow in water or on leaves. Iguanas eat them.

Bull – A male rhino or male giraffe.

Camouflage – Colours or patterns that help animals hide from predators.

Calf – A baby rhino or elephant.

Collective noun – A special word for a group of animals, like a dazzle of zebras.

Dazzle – A group of zebras.

Detach: To drop or let go. Baby iguanas detach their tails to escape predators.

Folivore – An animal that mostly eats leaves, like a sloth.

Herbivore – An animal that eats plants.

Hump – A fatty bump on a camel's back used for storing energy.

Iguana – A type of lizard that can climb trees, swim, and regrow its tail.

Keratin – The hard material that rhino horns and our fingernails are made from.

Nocturnal – Animals that are active at night, like skunks.

Porcupette – A baby porcupine.

Prickle – A group of porcupines.

Rosettes – The name for leopard spots because they look like little roses.

Savanna – A grassy plain with a few trees, home to elephants, giraffes, and zebras.

Stench – A group of skunks (also means a very bad smell).

Trunk – The long nose of an elephant used for smelling and grabbing things.

Tusks – Long teeth that grow from an elephant's mouth.

Water buffalo – A type of buffalo that lives in rivers or swamps and helps humans with farming.

Wrinkly skin – Skin with folds or wrinkles, like an elephant's, which helps it stay cool.

Can you remember what a group of skunks is called?
Turn back to page 21 to check if you were right!

About the Author

Stephanie was born on the Wirral and now lives in Nottingham with her husband, daughter, dogs, rabbits and hamster. She is an optician but when she is not testing eyes she can be found sewing, playing the harp, practising sign language, singing and/or adventuring with her family.

Can you remember what a group of dragons is called?

Turn back to page 23 to check if you were right!

If you enjoyed A Tower of Giraffes, look out for our other collective noun books:

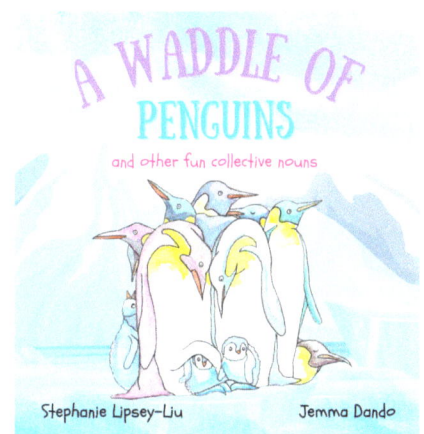
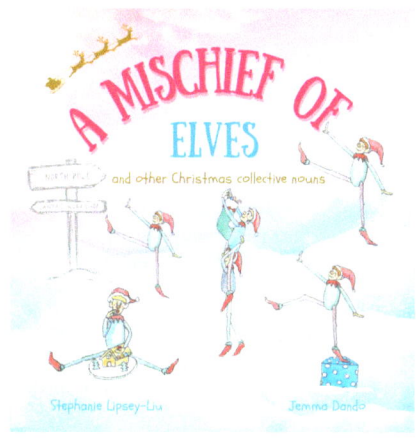

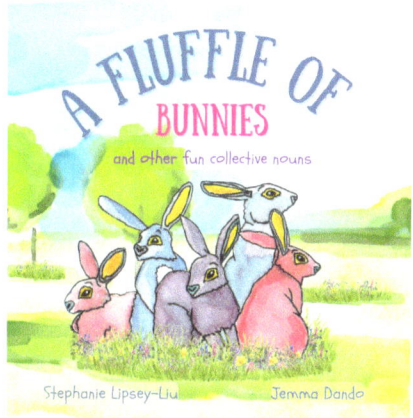

We would LOVE it if you could leave us a review on Amazon!

Ask your grown-up to help you write it.

If you'd like to share a picture of yourself reading any of our books, tag us on Facebook @littlelionpublishinguk or Instagram @littlelionpublishing.

www.ingramcontent.com/pod-product-compliance
Lightning Source LLC
Chambersburg PA
CBHW041120070526
44584CB00002B/224